THE COMPLEX LIVES OF
MEERKATS

BY SAMANTHA S. BELL

The Child's World®
childsworld.com

Published by The Child's World®
1980 Lookout Drive • Mankato, MN 56003-1705
800-599-READ • www.childsworld.com

Photographs ©: Kuttelvaserova Stuchelova/Shutterstock Images, cover, 1; Red Line Editorial, 5; Villiers Steyn/Shutterstock Images, 6; Dean Bertoncelj/iStockphoto, 8; Rodenberg Photography/Shutterstock Images, 9; iStockphoto, 10; Public Domain, 12; Ann & Steve Toon/NHPA/Photoshot/ Newscom, 13; Martina Berg/iStockphoto, 14; Marie Dirgova/Shutterstock Images, 17; blickwinkel/Alamy, 18; EcoPic/iStockphoto, 20

ISBN 9781503816244

LCCN 2016945620

Printed in the United States of America
PA02319

TABLE OF
CONTENTS

FAST FACTS

Name

- Meerkat (*Suricata suricatta*)

Diet

- Meerkats eat beetles, snails, scorpions, millipedes, small rodents, birds, lizards, roots, and fruit.
- Meerkats get all the water they need from their food.

Average Life Span

- Meerkats live for approximately eight years.

Size

- Meerkats' heads and bodies measure from 9.75 to 11.75 inches (24.8–29.8 cm). Their tails are between 7.5 and 9.6 inches (19–24 cm) long.
- Female meerkats tend to be slightly larger than male meerkats.

Weight

- Adult meerkats usually weigh less than 2.2 pounds (1 kg).

Where They're Found

- Meerkats live in the Kalahari Desert in southern Africa.

Meerkat habitats

Chapter 1

WATCH OUT!

A group of meerkats spreads out across the Kalahari Desert sand. They are looking for food. Some sniff the ground and scurry around. Others dig with their long claws. A group of meerkats is called a mob. This mob is tracking down insects and lizards hiding in the sand.

One of the meerkats finds a millipede. The millipede is covered in **toxins**. The meerkat rolls the millipede in the sand. The sand removes the toxins. Now the millipede is safe to eat. The meerkat pops it in its mouth.

Two meerkats, one male and one female, are not searching for food. The female climbs up on top of a large termite mound. The male climbs up high into a bush. These two meerkats are the lookouts for the mob.

◄ A meerkat digs for food. Meerkats have protective layers over their eyes that help keep dirt out.

▲ The lookout meerkat is the first to emerge to check to see if the area is safe.

The lookouts stand upright on their hind legs. Their heads swivel around as they watch for danger.

Suddenly one of the lookouts sees a hawk flying overhead. He lets out a sharp, **shrill** call. The sound means there is danger in the air. The other meerkats scatter into nearby **bolt-holes**. The bolt-holes have wide entrances. Several meerkats can fit through each hole opening at once. The meerkats are safe underground. They peek out of the openings.

The hawk flies away. One lookout leads the meerkats out of their holes. Next the **dominant** female emerges.

There are 10 meerkats in the mob. Along with the dominant female, there is a dominant male. There are also other females and young males.

Two different meerkats move into position as lookouts. They scan the horizon for predators such as eagles, jackals, and vultures. The meerkats have a different sound for each predator. Now the lookouts make a low peeping sound. They are telling the others that everything is safe.

▲ Meerkats have dark patches around their eyes that help them see well in the bright sun.

Chapter 2

DAILY LIFE

The meerkats live together in a burrow made of rooms and tunnels. In the morning, they make their way to the entrance. They quickly come out one by one. Once outside, the meerkats stand on their hind legs and face the sun. They have thin fur and dark skin on their stomachs. This helps the meerkats take in the sun's heat more quickly. After they have warmed up, the meerkats sit and **groom** each other. They chew ticks and other parasites off each other's backs and necks.

Next the mob is ready to **forage**. They will search for food most of the day. The meerkats scamper farther and farther from the burrow. But they are not far from safety. The ground is pocked with thousands of bolt-holes.

◀ **Meerkats have only a thin layer of fur on their bellies. This allows them to warm up quickly in the sun.**

The meerkats know the location of each bolt-hole in their territory.

During the hottest part of the day, some of the meerkats nap in the burrow. The others nap, play, and groom each other outside in the shade. A lookout keeps watch. Then it is time to forage again.

The group returns to their burrow before sunset. Each goes in through one of the 60 entrance holes. The first meerkat into the burrow meets a ground squirrel.

▲ Meerkats lay belly down in the shade to cool down and keep from overheating.

▲ A meerkat and a ground squirrel (left)
share a burrow. The two animals have
many of the same predators.

Ground squirrels live in the burrow, too. They are the
ones that dug the burrow.

The ground squirrel turns around and goes another
way. The meerkats move through the tunnels to a
sleeping room deep underground. They huddle
together to stay warm during the cold desert night.

Chapter 3

FAMILY LIFE

The dominant female is pregnant. Seventy days have passed since she became pregnant. While the other meerkats sleep, the female goes into another room in the burrow. She gives birth to four pups.

The mother meerkat begins to **nurse** the four babies. Sometimes other females nurse them, too. The mother needs a lot of energy to make the milk. She leaves the burrow to find more food. But she does not leave her pups alone. Another meerkat from the mob watches them. It stays close to the pups to make sure they are safe. It will not get to hunt until the next day. Then another meerkat will watch the babies.

◀ **Female meerkats are often forced to nurse the dominant female's pups.**

The pups grow in the burrow. After three weeks, the adults start to bring them solid food. The babies munch on chewed-up insects. They are still nursing, so the mother must keep eating more food than usual.

A week later, the pups wander outside for the first time. They stay close to the burrow with an adult meerkat. The adult stands upright, watching for danger. A yellow **mongoose** comes toward the babies. Usually, the mongoose is not a threat. But it might harm the pups. The adult chases the mongoose away through the sand.

Now that the pups can leave the burrow, the dominant female leads the mob to a clean burrow. There are five burrows in the mob's territory. The other meerkats follow the dominant female. Adult meerkats carry the pups to their new home.

The pups are eight weeks old. They go with the adults to forage. An adult helps each pup. One adult removes the stinger from a scorpion. Now the pup can catch the scorpion and eat it.

Another helper brings a lizard to a pup. The lizard starts to run away, but the helper brings it back. By four months old, the pups start hunting on their own.

▲ **Meerkats move to new burrows soon after pups are born. The pups must be carried to travel the long distances.**

Chapter 4

MEERKAT TERRITORY

One of the four young meerkats starts to dig. It makes a hole approximately 6 inches (15 cm) deep. It finds a beetle. Another meerkat eats a snail. Two meerkats communicate with purring sounds. They are working together to catch a lizard that is hiding in its burrow. One meerkat digs at the entrance. The other meerkat keeps watch in case the lizard tries to escape.

The meerkats change where they hunt every day. They mark their territory with their scent to keep other meerkat groups away. But another meerkat mob ignores the boundaries. One of the lookouts lets out a warning sound. The group gathers together to defend their territory. The two mobs try to scare each other.

◀ Older meerkats teach the young pups how to hunt and forage.

▲ Meerkats stay in groups to scare away
predators, such as the puff adder.

They line up across from one another. They raise their
tails straight up. Then they run toward each other. They
arch their backs and kick in the air.

This time the other group backs down. The other
meerkats turn around and move in the other direction.

The mob has defended its territory. They will not have to fight. The sun is about to set. The meerkats head toward their new burrow. But there is a **puff adder** near the entrance. This poisonous snake might kill one of the pups. The meerkats bunch together. They wave their tails in the air to distract the snake. Five of the meerkats attack. They bite the snake wherever they can. The snake lashes out, but then it quickly slithers away.

The mob huddles together in the burrow. They fall asleep. Tomorrow will be another busy day.

THINK ABOUT IT

- What do you think would happen to a meerkat that lived alone?
- How is a meerkat that watches pups similar to a human babysitter?
- Many people think meerkats are cute. Why do you think they would not make good pets?
- Do you think a meerkat mob could live in your backyard or a neighborhood park? Why or why not?

GLOSSARY

bolt-holes (BOHLT-HOHLS): Bolt-holes are openings in the ground into which an animal can run for safety. Meerkats know where the closest bolt-holes are.

dominant (DOM-uh-nunt): To be dominant is to control or rule. The dominant male and female in the meerkat group will have pups together.

forage (FOR-ij): To forage is to search for food. Meerkats forage most of the day.

groom (GROOM): To groom means to clean, brush, and make something tidy. Meerkats often groom each other.

mongoose (MON-goos): A mongoose is a quick-moving mammal with a long, slender body and long tail. The mongoose tries to attack the meerkat pups.

nurse (NURS): To nurse means to feed a baby with the mother's milk. The mother meerkat will nurse her pups.

puff adder (PUF A-der): A puff adder is a poisonous African snake that hisses loudly. The puff adder tries to attack the meerkat.

shrill (SHRIL): A noise that is shrill is high-pitched and piercing. The meerkat let out a shrill warning sound.

toxins (TOK-sins): Toxins are poisons made by an organism. Meerkats remove the toxins from millipedes before eating them.

TO LEARN MORE

Books

Gregory, Josh. *Meerkats.* New York: Children's Press, 2016.

Hesper, Sam. *Ground Squirrels.* New York: PowerKids, 2015.

O'Mara, John. *Mongooses.* New York: Gareth Stevens, 2015.

Web Sites

Visit our Web site for links about meerkats:
childsworld.com/links

Note to Parents, Teachers, and Librarians: We routinely verify our Web links to make sure they are safe and active sites. So encourage your readers to check them out!

SELECTED BIBLIOGRAPHY

Macdonald, David. *Meerkats.* London: New Holland, 1999. Print.

"Meerkat." *National Geographic.* National Geographic Society, 2016. Web. 30 Jun. 2016.

"Meerkat Biology and Behaviour." *Kalahari Meerkats.* Kalahari Meerkat Project, 3 Jun. 2007. Web. 30 Jun. 2016.

Nicholls, Henry. "The Truth about Meerkats." *BBC.com.* BBC, 24 Mar 2015. Web. 30 Jun. 2016.

INDEX

ABOUT THE AUTHOR

Samantha S. Bell has written more than 35 nonfiction books for children. Animals are one of her favorite topics to write about. She earned her bachelor's degree and teaching certification from Furman University. She is a workshop and conference speaker, creative writing teacher, and enthusiastic student of all things nature.